The Job Nobody Dreams Of

The Job Nobody Dreams Of

Written by
Bill Becker

Platypus Publishing

PLATYPUS
PUBLISHING

Table of Contents

Acknowledgments

Just as being a successful salesperson is a team effort, so is a book. The idea is mine. Most of the stories are mine. The smart-ass commentary is definitely mine, but there is so much more behind the scenes that happened to make this book ready for public consumption.

I found that writing a book on something I am passionate about is a little like raising a child. As a father of five, I know of what I speak!

First, my editor Chandi Lyn. Was she a pain in my ass? Without question. Did she use up all the red ink on the internet to mark up each chapter? She sure did. Was she the greatest thing to happen to me and my book? Absolutely yes! She did exactly what I asked of her: clean up my mess and make me look like a decent writer. The ability to bounce ideas off of her was invaluable, and her suggestions made this a much better book than I could have ever dreamed of before I started.

Ben Watson, who was head of sales for several years at my last job, was my favorite boss of all time. We worked on many customer strategies and had several memorable email exchanges and strategy sessions. He always had my back and was the epitome of "figuring shit out." He defined what a great sales manager should be.

To the salespeople who shared their experiences with me, I appreciate your knowledge. It greatly enhanced this book.

To all my former coworkers, we typically spent more time with each other than with our families. The reality is we were family as well. We laughed, cried, and fought, but in the end, we always supported each other and understood that the combination of all our talents made us unbeatable. The one thing (the only thing!) I miss about retirement is the daily interaction with you all.

Finally, I spent considerable time in the book talking about the importance of coworkers, but one stood out, my loyal companion of 16 years, Baxter. Every coworker and client would eventually learn about the goofy dude sleeping to my left in my home office. Many conversations started out not by asking how I was doing but with, "How's our boy?" I am so freaking grateful that I got to work from home for the last 10 years of his life.

About the Author

Bill Becker never dreamed of becoming a salesperson. Growing up, he was determined to become either a veterinarian or a radio disc jockey. Eventually, he joined his hometown radio station to sell radio advertising. After 16 years in radio sales, where he developed numerous groundbreaking programs to capture non-traditional revenue, he moved into IT sales and consulting. In IT and consulting, he signed multitudinous high-profile software clients over a 20-year career. Bill also enjoys using Dictionary.com to find words to make him look more photosynthesis—he doesn't always use them correctly.

After retiring at the end of 2022, Bill now expounds on the attributes of sales careers and advocates for homeless initiatives.

During his free time, Bill plays basketball, writes and performs comedy, and gets up to whatever mayhem comes across his path, including writing this book.

Introduction

As long as you're still alive,
you always have the chance to start again.

Author Emily Acker
from the book *No Longer Broken*

Monday, November 23rd, 2015, started like most days. I got up, fed the cat and dog, had breakfast, and got dressed. Then I went off script. I took my dog Baxter to the vet, telling them I was boarding him for a few days. Then I texted a friend to find him a good home. My tasks done, I headed to the Creek Turnpike bridge. My life was in its finale.

I call that day "my bad day" (you can read about it at https://tinyurl.com/MyCarlsbad). While it was a truly awful day, it was also the first day of the rest of my life.

At this point in my life, my career had mostly focused on sales—16 years in radio sales and 15 years in IT sales—but after my wake-up call, sales allowed me to rebuild my life and change the lives of many others.

Right after 9/11, I worked with many displaced workers. These workers came from all kinds of backgrounds, and after taking stock of the situation, it dawned on me that none of these people came from sales!

It also occurred to me that no one grows up dreaming of becoming a salesperson. And voila! A book was born.

If you are skeptical about salespeople and what a career in sales looks like, this is the book for you!

I self-published a similar book with the same title as this one. That 2002 version of the book was poorly done (though the remaining copies might be worth a fortune on eBay after I am gone!), but the message is the same today as it was back then. A sales career can help you rebuild your life.

I know firsthand. Whatever reason you have for reading this book, know that you are in the right place. You might be unemployed or underemployed and looking for a way to create a better life for yourself and your family. You might just be here for a lark! If you promise to keep reading, I will promise to make it worth your time.

I've made mistakes, and I've had tremendous success. In this book, you'll learn about both! You'll read how I landed my first-ever sales job at my hometown radio station after years of being turned down. You will learn about making connections and pursuing your goals as well as what not to do on your first day at work.

This book represents lessons learned over several decades of insanity and persistence. I often joke that I never made any money off my looks or personality, but I am tenacious as hell. I have made many mistakes and often tell my kids that mistakes are great life lessons. If you get something right, you may have just been lucky. If you make a mistake, you learn what not to do next time.

The investor and entrepreneur Naval Ravikant said, "To write a great book, you must first become the book." I don't know if this is a great book, but I lived everything you will read here, so, you could say I became the book.

Ultimately, a career in sales puts you in front of a lot of people. **If you are good at what you do, people will notice, and being noticed will open many other doors.**

Years ago, I had a family friend who sold men's clothing. One of his customers was in the oil and gas business. The friend got hired as a salesperson and ultimately became a senior VP and was able to retire several years later (well before 65!).

You never know where life will take you. Did you ever think you would read a book about sales careers? Did you ever dream of becoming a salesperson?

One final note…

I spent the last year of my career and the first six months of retirement thinking about what this book should be and how things have changed since I wrote that first version 20 years ago. Much of that deliberation was spent deciding what not to include, so I didn't waste your time.

I put myself in your shoes and thought, "What do I need to know?" and "Why is this important?" I was surprised when the page count ended up being fewer than 200 pages.

Then I thought, who cares!

- Did I present everything that was relevant to someone new to sales? Yep!

- Did I provide a roadmap to go out and get your first sales job (even if a company wasn't hiring at the moment)? Absolutely yes!

Then who cares about the page count! If this book was 400 pages, you probably wouldn't finish it; I probably wouldn't either.

If, after finishing the book, you decide you would like additional help, including weekly Q&A sessions with guest lecturers and myself, there is a companion course you can purchase. To find more information, check out my website. For now, the book contains everything you need to change your life.

So, keep reading, take notes on the parts that apply to your life, ignore the sarcasm, and embrace the randomness that led you to this point in your life. Because the lessons I've learned can guide you, or someone you know, to build a better life. You just have to listen.

Chapter 1

Why This Book

---

*At the end of the day, it's not about what you
have or even what you've accomplished.
It's about what you've done
with those accomplishments.
It's about who you've lifted up,
who you've made better.
It's about what you've given back.*

Author Denzel Washington
from the book *A Hand to Guide Me*

When I was younger, I wanted fame and fortune. When I started raising kids, fortune became a little more critical (you think?!). I did seek fame for a while when I started a sports-comedy webcast called Weekend Sports Update (think fake news on SNL but just sports) in 2012. Before social media took off, I managed to get over two million views between YouTube and Vimeo within two and a half years.

Then I got divorced and shit wasn't funny anymore, so I stopped. I stopped everything.

I was given a second chance at life and found myself building an incredible career in sales.

When I retired in November of 2022, I still had another year left in me. I loved my clients, my coworkers, and my life. I was walking away from a lucrative career where I was making over $500,000 a year because I didn't love the changes our new private equity owners were implementing. I also wanted to use my superpowers to help end homelessness (because I am bold enough to think I can make a difference), so I called it a career. You can learn more about my homeless manifesto over at ConnectTheDots.cc.

When I retired, I wrote a long message to my coworkers about what they meant to me and all the things my job allowed me to do. That particular job (and the part my coworkers played) was the means for my personal and professional accomplishments. Sales allowed me to do everything I wanted to do in this latest chapter of my life, including proselytizing about sales careers.

My smart-ass attitude and sassy disposition—a hallmark of Weekend Sports Update—still plays a significant role in my life, whether it's evangelizing sales careers or garnering attention on serious issues like unhoused peoples in the U.S.

My experience has led me to understand that sales is not the career people dream about when they are younger, but it is a career that can make dreams come true.

Five years ago, I came across an article on Medium by John Gorman titled *Happiness is Overrated.* It seemed like obvious clickbait, but I also had to see what this guy was talking about with his catchy title. It changed my life. In his article, Gorman shares the high points of his incredible life and also the fear that engulfs him. The consuming fear that he could lose it all in an instant.

He was collecting happiness…always looking to add to his bucket. Instead, he concluded that, "Once we have peace, we will no longer need to seek happiness." Maybe that was some new-age psychobabble, but it really hit home for me. Happiness, like most emotions, is fleeting. There are days you will be happy and days you won't be. However, if you are chasing that happiness, you are almost guaranteed to have down days.

I know there were times that I would worry—as a parent, worry feels like a constant companion! What if they break a bone? Will they make friends? etc. But financial worries, like school supplies, clothes, electric bills, food, etc., are a different kind of stress. This stress can be mitigated. My kids are all grown now, but I have peace of mind that if something financial comes up, I've got it covered.

It's the same thing with my dog Baxter who beat two types of cancer and was losing the use of his back legs when he finally passed away. Spending tens of thousands of dollars to keep your dog alive is not ideal, but the only thing worse is not having the money to do it. Because of my job, I was able to tell my vet, "Do whatever it takes, regardless of the cost."

You have your own worries, some of which might be similar to mine. Whatever they are, they are real. They are valid. They are yours. Life is hard enough, and when you add not being able to provide things most of us take for granted—like food or housing or just being able to go out to eat once a month—life sucks.

That's what this book is, a prescription for a life that sucks!

Not having a job sucks. Not having a good job sucks. Worrying about your future and possible layoffs sucks. The Phoenix Suns suck…sorry that's my Dallas Mavericks fandom being a smartass.

Having a good job allows you to take care of your needs. Having a great job lets you give back and help others. There is a unique type of joy that comes from changing a life other than your own.

One of my most memorable moments involved a family from Memphis. They had a rough time and were about to have their brand-new puppy put down. I came across a Facebook fundraiser, and they hadn't raised much money. Worse yet, there were just a couple of days left. I contacted the Memphis police directly, took care of all the fines and fees, and the dog was returned to the family the next day. A picture of the little girl and her dog sits in my living room.

Nobel-Prize-Winning author Toni Morrison used to tell her students, "Just remember that your real job is that if you are free, you need to free somebody else. If you have some power, then your job is to empower somebody else."

That's what I want to do. I want to give back. I want to inspire people who have fallen on hard times and show them there is hope! You can rebuild your life and get a job that allows you to earn good money and be proud of what you do for a living.

My story isn't unique; that's why you will hear stories of other salespeople throughout the book. This book is a deeper dive into the details of how someone can follow in my footsteps. I'm an idiot (just ask people!), and I did it.

Am I being entirely altruistic? Well, not completely. My life experience is valuable, so a book is a cheap way to teach others how to start anew, to create a good life while also rewarding myself for my years of sales experience. It's a win-win for sure. I truly hope you will find value in the following pages. That you will be inspired. That you will walk back from the ledge and begin again. Because you can.

Why should you choose sales?

Despite what you might think and have heard, sales is a dream job. People don't understand this because there's so much crap out there about sales and the people who sell.

It's human nature to mock what you don't understand. It's also an easy trap to fall into painting an entire industry or field based on a single bad experience.

It stands to reason that there are bad apples out there, especially when many consider sales as a job of last resort ("I'm doing this until something better comes along"). Just like there are bad plumbers, accountants, and auto mechanics, there are bad salespeople. This just creates an amazing opportunity for you!

I love basketball, but if I played against an NBA player, I would get my ass kicked. However, if I went and played against an average middle schooler, I would smoke them! That's really what happened in my sales career...I was going up against middle schoolers. I was one of those salespeople who stood out.

I was nothing special. No college education, bearing a vague resemblance to George Clooney, and an understanding of what it really took to be successful. Okay, maybe that middle attribute was a stretch, but I quickly figured out what it took to be successful in sales. Keep reading to find out.

Using this book.

Now, we must do some quick housekeeping...I know, it's not my favorite thing either. But, alas, it must be done.

In this book, you will find some additional help beyond the standard informational content. At the end of each chapter, I will highlight that chapter's key points in the **chapter takeaways** section. Throughout the book, you will also find **sidebars**, **Q&As**, and **Pro tips**.

A **sidebar** is something that I want you to know, but maybe doesn't actually fit in the text.

Q&A notes are bonuses. I asked several successful salespeople a series of questions. This section is where you will learn from their experiences—because everyone needs a break from my ramblings. Each chapter will highlight one of these incredible people and give you a snapshot of their careers in sales.

Pro tips are insider secrets. These are ideas and tips to help you jump in like a pro from the start.

Chapter takeaways!

- I've seen and done a lot.
- I've been broke and made my fortune.
- I had my brief shining moment of fame.
- Sales is an excellent career.

- One of the most important lessons I've learned is that a good job impacts people beyond their paycheck. A good job gives people peace of mind, and peace is everything.

Chapter 2

Why Sales

---

*Being in sales will be the most challenging,
but also the most rewarding
career you could ever have!
Don't listen to the negative hype
about sales. It's not true!*

Krista Ketchmark
Vice President, IT Business Development at Pearson VUE

Let's start with a little pop quiz. Name a career field that doesn't involve sales. Fine art? Social services? Nonprofits? Healthcare? They all require a certain amount of selling because everything revolves around sales.

Artists sell their work—often through an agent or gallery. Social services and nonprofits fundraise constantly! My doctor tries to sell me on the idea of giving up Pop-Tarts. He sucks as a salesman. I'm not giving them up. Somedays Pop-Tarts are the only thing that keeps me from taking hostages.

What about everyday life? With apologies to Jeff Foxworthy, here are some signs that you just might be a salesperson…

- If you have tried convincing your wife that watching The Godfather on A&E for the ninety-fourth time is a better movie choice than the latest chick flick… you might be a salesperson.

- If, when you were a kid, you tried to convince your mom that her favorite crystal ornament was not broken during a fight with your brother, that it was actually broken years before you were even born…you just might be a salesperson. By the way, I did not close that particular sale. Early lesson to not lie during a deal.

- If you've asked someone out on a date, you just might be a salesperson. I know, I know. I can hear your guffaw from here. But think about it; dating is sales! In both instances, you are building rapport and finding points of commonality.

> **Sidebar:** If you took your date out to a nice dinner and then a fancy wine bar, only to drop her off at her boyfriend's house afterward, you need to qualify your leads a little better! That's a true story about my first post-divorce date.

- Finally, if you have ever applied for a job or asked for a raise or promotion, you just might be a salesperson. You were selling yourself, and that's all anyone does in a sale.

Meet Krista Ketchmark

Bill: What did you want to be when you were growing up?

Krista: I wanted to be a forest ranger, a zookeeper, or a veterinarian.

Bill: What did you do before you went into sales and what/who got you into sales?

Krista: I was in operations working as a product manager and then as a program manager. Our Vice President of Sales approached me to join their sales team. I wrinkled up my nose at the thought. I replied indignantly, "I'm not a salesperson!" The VP didn't let the idea go and spent nine months recruiting me. Now that I've been working on their team for over 10 years, I realize they used all their sales skills to recruit me!

Sales myths we all know.

What's the first thing you think of when you think of a salesperson? Pushy or high pressure, manipulative, sneaky? While you might have a negative image of salespeople, you also probably think, "They make a lot of money." All of the characterizations are true! Just like there are good and bad lawyers or accountants or plumbers, there are good and bad salespeople.

> **Bill:** What's the craziest thing that's happened in your sales career?
> **Krista:** When I left operations, my colleagues told me I was going to the dark side, and one person said they could never be in sales because they're not a good liar. Wow! I've never lied or felt I was on the dark side as a salesperson.

It's also true that sales is a career where you can make a lot of money.

In sales, as in any profession, it's essential to separate fact from fiction. Let's go over some of the common myths about salespeople.

You have to be a people person. Nope! Another common refrain I hear is, "Salespeople are born, not made." It does help if you are personable, but many good salespeople have dry personalities, are introverts, or feel inadequate in their conversational skills and still excel at sales through their professionalism.

13

Bill: How is sales different from what you were expecting? What surprised you about your current job?

Krista: I didn't expect to love being in sales as much as I do. I feel closer to our customers and empowered to be their champion, as well as closer to our business. It's an incredibly rewarding career professionally, personally, and financially. Being in sales has completely changed my life and the lives of my family.

Customers don't want to deal with salespeople. Wrong! Prospects will do their initial research online but often want or need to talk to a live person who can answer specific questions and (this is the key) offer advice. Good salespeople are considered business advisors, equal in stature to a company's legal or finance team. Your customers want and need your advice.

You must be an expert on your product. Ne! (I love Google Translate.) You certainly need to know the basics of what you are selling, but you don't need to know the product or service inside out. It's good to know the talking points, like how the product helps solve a problem or how it can benefit your client, but you don't need to be an expert. I came from IT sales and saw numerous technical experts fail miserably when they tried to sell because they focused solely on features.

People only buy on price. Perhaps, but only if you are doing it wrong. People buy on value. Price is merely a factor in the buying process. Today, you can get a 65" TV (yeah, they still make them that small!) for $300. You could also pay $3,000+ for the same size. If you can help your client solve a problem, you'll spend little time discussing the cost. The price only becomes the default decision-making criterion if you don't clearly show how your solution will help your customer.

Overcoming objections is the most critical skill. Puh-lease! Listening is the most important skill. Why are they talking to you? What do they really need? You will fail if all you do is offer up memorized responses to a prospect's questions. Listen first.

Social selling is the key to fame and fortune. Yeah, no. Social selling can effectively get you to buy $90 gym shorts (damn you, Instagram!), but if your product or service requires salespeople, social selling isn't the secret sauce.

You have to make cold calls. Stop It! You don't have to spend all day making cold calls. Now, you do need to prospect, but that can happen in a variety of ways. By the way, most of us won't answer the phone even when we know who's calling (sorry, Mom!). Cold calling is dead because it can cheapen your brand and tank your credibility. There are hundreds of books, courses, and opinions on prospecting. I am here to tell you to relax. It's 2023; you don't need to call strangers unless you are ordering delivery.

What does it take to get a great job?

Historically, what did it take to get a great job? You often needed a college degree and several years of experience in a specific field to command great pay and benefits. When you lose that job, you were typically faced with two options:

1. Stay in your profession and move to another city, uprooting your family and incurring thousands of dollars in moving expenses in the process.

2. Stay in your current city, change professions, and start from scratch. Many people who get laid off go back to school. In addition to not having an income, they use up their savings while working on a degree—an activity that does not guarantee anything. A 2021 study by Experian showed that 30 percent of recent college graduates moved in with their parents (with another 31 percent moving back to their hometown for cheaper rent). People with shiny new degrees who are young enough that they won't command a high salary are struggling to find work; how much more difficult will it be for someone older with dusty old degrees (or no degrees)? Which leads to an unpleasant reality…

Unemployment in later years can be devastating.

If you are changing industries and are over the age of thirty-five, not only do you have to find a job, but you'll also be forced to deal with an unspoken age bias. There is a particular cruelty that joblessness inflicts on older adults. Many are hunting for work for the first time in decades. They are limited in their flexibility to move because they are pressured to provide for their children or elderly parents, or they just really like their city. Even if they secure employment, they often end up with a starting wage more appropriate for someone in their early twenties.

Now that we've covered the negative aspects of finding a new job, let's go over the attributes of the perfect job and then dive into why sales checks off every box for someone looking to land a new gig.

Attributes of the perfect job.

If you created the perfect job, what would it look like? No, you can't say it's one of those no-show jobs the mob gives some of its members. It could, however, look like this:

- **No experience is necessary.** You aren't going to be disqualified because you don't have 5-10 years of experience.

- **No education requirements**. You don't have the time, resources, or desire to go back to school. You need to generate an income now!
- **Great pay**. Many jobs are going unfilled today (early 2023) because they don't pay a living wage. You want more than the bare minimum, and you don't want to wait for annual pay raises or stock options to vest just to be able to keep up with inflation.
- **Little competition for positions**. You don't want to go up against 300 people for a single opening. Searching for employment and trying to get an interview can often rob someone of their dignity.
- **Your age isn't important.** I mentioned this earlier. Age discrimination is illegal, yet it happens every single day. The perfect job has no age barrier.

Okay, let's be clear, there is no such thing as the perfect job. There is, however, a career with attributes that are as close as you can get to defining the perfect job. Let's go back over the list and look at it through the eyes of someone considering a sales career.

> **Bill:** Describe your typical day.
> **Krista:** My typical day is spent wearing multiple hats in customer-facing meetings and internal meetings, mostly virtual, but some in-person. A typical day requires me to use my uber problem-

solving skills and negotiation skills, all with a high degree of diplomacy. I'm the voice of our customers in all meetings but in order to maintain credibility and trust both externally and internally, I must balance being a customer champion with being a good corporate citizen.

Why sales is the perfect second career!

No experience necessary! Since the no-experience element is one of the key features of *The Job Nobody Dreams Of,* we will spend some time on the subject. Sure, companies like to hire salespeople with previous sales experience, but the characteristics that make a great salesperson do not have to be mastered in a previous sales job. In this book, you'll hear from successful salespeople who were project managers, teachers, and taxi drivers. Being a great listener, possessing a tenacious attitude, and being able to ask questions and pay attention to the answers are attributes that can be developed in any background.

The new economy requires better salespeople and better doesn't always mean more experienced. Someone with 10 years of order-taking experience is far less valuable to a company than a new-to-sales person who can produce a new book of business and create new revenue streams.

No education requirements! There are no degrees in sales (Business Administration doesn't count). Sales education comes from studying and learning by doing—often learning from your mistakes. As an established salesman, I always made a point to give a new sales rep a few of my smaller accounts. That way, they could get in "reps" (like batting practice or free throw shooting in sports) to practice their craft and learn the business. In sales, you learn on the job.

Great pay! Outside of sports stars and entertainers, sales is one of the highest-paying jobs available, and for most sales reps there are no caps! Sales compensation plans vary from company to company, ranging from straight commission to a draw (salary) plus commission. I have seen sales newbies become the top salesperson in the company in their second or third month. One other point concerning pay, sales is one of the few jobs where you can make more money than your boss! Most sales managers are paid some form of salary and bonus. Outside of my first radio job back during the Mesozoic Era, I always earned more than my boss.

Little competition for positions! In good times or bad, there are always sales positions available. While I won't say salespeople never get laid off, it's unlikely for a good producer to be let go. Layoffs are a result of a company trying to cut expenses. It's not too smart to ditch the folks bringing in the revenue.

> **Pro tip:** While you will find numerous sales position listings on online job boards and company websites, many managers like to hire referred candidates from customers or their current staff. Just because you don't see an opening listed for a particular company doesn't mean they aren't hiring!

Your age doesn't matter! Look, if you are 64 years old and seeking a job to keep you busy for one more year, yeah, it will be tough to find someone willing to hire you. However, many companies would love to have you if you are willing to commit to several years—age can be a benefit here! One thing older workers have is life experience, as well as a professional network of contacts. Contacts that could open doors to new sales. So as long as you are old enough to work legally, age shouldn't be a barrier here.

More reasons to consider a sales career!

Sales is the one job you can get even if a company isn't hiring! Top managers are always looking for great salespeople and will hire someone even if they don't currently have an opening. I've been hired multiple times during my career by a company that wasn't hiring at the time. In addition, I have designed my own job, presented it to a company, and been hired for this newly created position! You'll learn about how I did that in Chapter 9.

There are great sales jobs, regardless of where you live! It used to be that you were limited to working where you lived, and you had to move to work for a company in another city or state. Today, more and more sales jobs are remote. There are sometimes strategic reasons to meet face-to-face with prospects, but the new norm in sales is virtual and working from anywhere you have a computer and the internet. You can talk to more clients each day and be much more effective when you cut out the daily commute. Plus, with so many clients being global, you can work in multiple time zones!

> **Sidebar:** You don't have to wear pants!

Years ago, a sales manager at my radio station said something profound. If you knew how to sell, you could throw a dart at a map, and wherever it landed, you could find a job to support yourself. You might not be selling something you were interested in or were passionate about, but you could get a job that would allow you to support yourself and your family.

That's still true today. And today, your options are even better!

With so many sales jobs being virtual, you can flip the script. If there is a company you want to work for, call them regardless of where you are located.

Sales offers the most quantifiable results! There is no daily wondering if you are performing well. You do not have to wait for your quarterly or annual performance review with your boss to learn where you stand. As a result of this accountability, you have the power to determine the outcome of your own career. This control simply doesn't exist in most jobs.

> **Bill:** You enter an elevator with your dream client who asks you what you do for a living. How do you respond?
>
> **Krista:** I lead our business development team, which is focused on customer advocacy and industry thought leadership.

You can make money selling even without a job!

You don't even need a product, let alone a company, to make money in sales. What?!? Sales is simply brokering a transaction for a good or service in exchange for money. I often think I could be a great movie producer with my skill set. Producers find a product (script, book, current event, etc.) and assemble a package to sell to a studio. Their commission is a producing fee and sometimes a movie revenue cut. Think about all the ways this principle might apply in other situations.

Most good employers have an employee referral program where you can earn $$$ for referring someone for a job opening. That concept can also apply to just about anything. What about referring a friend to a real estate broker or business associate to your banker? If there's a transaction, you can ask for a referral fee. The same goes for any introduction you make with your personal and professional contacts. Monetize your network. Create a simple agreement (or automate it through an app such as Introducely), and whenever you feel you can add value by introducing different parties, ask for your cut! Think about the companies you already do business with; do they want more customers? Of course! Will they pay you to refer business to them? You don't know if you don't ask! To quote Wayne Gretzky, "You miss 100% of the shots you don't take."

Chapter takeaways!

- Everything is sales. Why not make money doing something you do anyway?
- There are no barriers to entry for a sales career. You can start tomorrow!
- You can get hired even if a company doesn't have any openings!
- Ability to work from anywhere!

Chapter 3

What Really Happens During a Sale

---

*My role doesn't really feel like selling.
It feels more like consulting
and helping clients and prospects solve problems
that need to be solved and finding creative
ways to address those needs.*

Eric Strause
Sr. Director, of Business Development at Skillable

What do you imagine happens during a sale? Do you think of a slick-talking salesperson trying to trick someone into signing a deal? Do you assume they are using high-pressure closing techniques taught by some guy like Alec Baldwin's character in *Glengarry Glen Ross*? The truth is that professional selling today is nothing like you see in the movies.

In my 20+ years in technology sales, I earned several million dollars. Not once did I ever convince someone that they needed my service. **Sales is not about convincing**—it's simply about having conversations. Really, really good conversations.

I found people who were already in the market and helped them see why I was the best choice to guide them. Simply put, I figured shit out. Let me explain.

In today's world, people do their own research before talking to a salesperson. The internet has made it easy to check out any product or service. Amazon reviews are an integral part of any purchasing decision, even if I end up purchasing it somewhere else. I am not proud that I once spent 20 minutes reading reviews for a pooper scooper. I had four dogs and it had to be the best!

For those products that do require additional research—usually, those with a mid- to long-term buying cycle—a salesperson is a welcome resource. A salesperson can give advice on how to implement a product or service, often sharing examples of similar customers who went through the same process. That's the basis of the axiom, "What can you do for me, and who else says so?"

In my previous job, I worked with software companies. It would carry a lot of weight when I could say Microsoft, IBM, Veritas, etc., were already customers. While I would obviously never share confidential information, I would share how current clients took their data (virtual labs) and onboarded them to my platform. My prospective clients loved that I had solid customers who gave us great reviews. They also appreciated it when I could explain how our product solved problems.

Knowing what to do is valuable. Do you know what's worth even more? Knowing what not to do!

People hesitate to make a purchasing decision because they don't want to make a mistake. Engaging with a salesperson/advisor who can help prospects navigate potential landmines gives them peace of mind. Peace of mind is what keeps price out of the discussion and makes saying yes easier.

Meet Eric Strause

Bill: What did you want to be when you were growing up?

Eric: I wanted to be an NHL hockey goalie as a child. As I got older, I wanted to be a teacher and went to college to do that.

Bill: What did you do before you went into sales and what/who got you into sales?

Eric: I worked for an IT Education company for 21 1/2 yrs. I started at the ground floor packing and shipping books to classes. I moved into Logistics and managed freight tracking. I then moved into product management, but it was really an education in operations, finance, and project management. I then shifted back to products and got heavily involved in supporting sales, especially field/enterprise sales supporting complex training programs and solutions. During this time, I spent 75% of my time on sales calls and helping sellers close deals, but I was not commissioned at all. I then moved into a Product Director role and lead teams supporting a mass of technology portfolios. At our peak, my team managed the portfolio that drove over 65% of the company revenues.

In 2018, I opted for a layoff to find my next role and knew I wanted to be an individual contributor in an enterprise sales role. I posted my focus to pursue a new role on Facebook and I was immediately contacted by a former colleague/peer who asked if I'd be interested in a sales role, he had an opening. We met for coffee, I flew the next week to see the CEO, and I flew home having accepted a position. I was 47 years old and making a career change to sales.

A typical sales cycle.

Let's talk about prospecting. You need to figure out who you want to talk to. What is their title or job role? In my case, since I was selling virtual labs for software training, it was typically someone with the title of Training Manager, Director of Training & Certification, or something similar.

You also need to know if other departments within a company might use your product or service. With virtual labs, it was typically the Training Department, Product Sales (our platform was used for product demonstrations), and Certification (professional exams). Once I figured that out, I learned what the titles of those department heads might be. That's who I needed to talk to.

If you are in Business-to-Business (B2B) sales, you will probably spend a lot of time on LinkedIn. You can search for connections by job titles, industries, and countless other search criteria. While my entire career was B2B, almost everything also applies to selling Direct-to-Consumer (D2C) or Business-to-Consumer (B2C). Where do you find those prospects? Ask your manager and/or coworkers.

You can also send messages through LinkedIn (there are numerous ways), or you can email the prospect directly if you know the company's email structure, e.g., firstname.lastname@company. com. Here is an example of a simple email I would send to a prospect ...

> **Pro tip:** Ask about lead generation during the interview process.

29

> *Good morning, Stephen,*
>
> *We are a EdTech company that helps software companies facilitate learning through hands-on lab experience, including Performance Based Tests for certification exams.*
>
> *Some of our current clients include Microsoft, AWS, Veritas, and IBM. I believe we could be great partners and an important resource for you and Chef Software.*
>
> *Could I get 10 minutes of your time to explain WHY I believe we would be a great combination?*

That email isn't very long (no one will read long emails), and I am only asking for 10 minutes. It also quickly tells the potential client who I am, what I can do for them, and why they should be interested.

Bill: Describe your typical day.

Eric: I check in on all my emails and meetings first thing in the morning. I generally try to make a short list of goals for the day. These are mainly key activities or tasks I need to check off my list. Most days, I work from home and have 4–8 calls, and I am constantly trying to move all of my opportunities to the next step by checking in with clients or internals to clear the obstacles to move it along. Creativity and problem-solving is what I enjoy most about my job.

Each message has four primary outcomes:

- They respond and are interested and want to meet.
- They don't respond but know a coworker who may be interested. They forward the message (sometimes including me in the forwarded message).
- They are interested but never open your email.
- They aren't interested and don't respond.

The following two outcomes happen, but are less likely:

- They are not interested today and don't respond but hang onto the email and reply months or even years later. I have had that happen on numerous occasions in my career.

- They actually reply to tell me they are not interested. That's the rarest of scenarios, and it's OK! I love it when a client says no. It means I don't waste my time bugging them about something they don't want.

Bill: You enter an elevator with your dream client who asks you what you do for a living. How do you respond?

Eric: I work for an EdTech company that helps organizations with solutions that support skills development and skills validation. It's an amazing organization that is rapidly growing and I am the happiest I've ever been in my entire career.

If you've been in the business world for a while and previously joined LinkedIn, you might already have a network of contacts. Some of your connections might be able to help you with introductions to a prospect. Others might know a guy who knows this other guy whose dog groomer knows a gal who runs a company…think six-degrees-of-Kevin-Bacon (Google it).

You might get leads from your marketing department, with the best ones being prospects that contacted your company for more information. Regardless of where the prospect came from, it is your job to schedule a first meeting.

The first meeting.

Everyone has ideas on how to schedule this meeting. There are a million scripts to follow and a million more pieces of advice. Listen and learn and then take all those ideas and mash them together to figure out your own. Here are a few methods I have found to be successful when asking for that first meeting:

- "Hi Jerry, I know you are busy, but I would love to get 10-15 minutes of your time to share what other companies just like yours are doing with us to multiply their customer training effectiveness. I promise not to waste your time!"
- Email Jerry a $25 gift card to a restaurant and say you'd like to buy him a virtual lunch where you can chat for 10-15 minutes.

Here are a couple of essential things to remember about initial client meetings, 98% of prospects (remember that 77% of statistics are made up on the fly) agree to a meeting because they are quite possibly interested in what you represent. If they had zero interest, they wouldn't have agreed to a meeting, which is good news. You don't want to waste your time. A prospect might not be interested enough to buy—and might never buy—but they had enough interest to take 10 minutes out of their day to chat.

Typically, you aren't closing the sale on this initial call. You are there to ask questions and listen. That's it! A sale usually requires a handful of meetings unless you are selling a low-cost product or service, or the customer has been warmed up ahead of time.

Pro tip: Always return messages on the same day or the next morning at the latest! I cannot tell you the number of times clients and prospects applauded me for returning messages quickly. Really!?? I thought that was my job, yet every week of my 30+ year career, I would get an email thanking me for my quick reply. I guess I am glad many salespeople don't do it because it made it easier for me to shine. If you don't have the answer to their question that day, email them anyway and tell them you are still working on their request. It's common courtesy that apparently isn't that common in the business world.

In this initial question-asking session, you want to discover a few things:

- Is the person you are talking to the decision maker for purchasing this product/service?
  - If not, who is?

- Whatever you are selling, you ask if they are already using a similar product or service.
  - If they are, "How are they using it? What do they like about it? What don't they like? Knowing this is the key to getting them to change.
  - If they aren't, are they considering starting to use a similar product or service in the future? Chances are they are; otherwise, they wouldn't have agreed to meet with you.
- You'll inquire about their timeline. Do they expect to make a decision this week, in the next 90 days, or later this year?
- Listen to everything they say and take notes. Did they mention having a spouse? Did they talk about their dog? Did you overhear any other conversations that may be important to remember for later?

Typically, you will know if the prospect will have technical folks on the call with them. How do you know? Because you are going to ask them ahead of time when you set the meeting up. If they have technical support on the call, they may have more detailed questions for you than a typical client. But don't stress! If you know the answer, great! If you don't, you simply say, "I don't know, but I will get back to you later today with the answer."

Pro tip: Never try to bullshit your way through a question you don't know the answer to! Recognizing and owning up to what you don't know doesn't make you look weak; it makes you look real. Being honest is more acceptable than getting caught in a lie, especially with a new prospect!

You'll wrap up this first meeting with an agreement to meet again or an agreement on when it's appropriate for you to reach out to schedule the next appointment. It might be for a demo, a technical discussion (at which time you can bring your own tech resource), or even to present your proposal.

You'll take what you learned in that meeting and write a summary. With me, it sometimes took a while because I had to decipher my handwriting! I can write much faster than I can type, but sometimes my chicken scratch requires mental gymnastics to figure out what I wrote. That's why it's good to write up the summary as soon as the meeting is over.

Boom! You just finished your first meeting. Did anything I just shared seem difficult? I don't think so; it's just two or more people having a discussion. It's not, as one of my former bosses used to say, rocket surgery.

Since you are brand new to sales, you probably wouldn't have done the meeting by yourself anyway. Usually, your boss or a fellow salesperson will go on a few calls with you. Good salespeople will also do practice calls before the real thing.

This is simply about asking questions. You can do it; everyone does it on a daily basis! What are we having for dinner tonight? Why are they called headphones if you don't use them to talk? Why is Eva Mendes still with Ryan Gosling? (Don't judge me!).

You are probably wondering, "What questions should I ask?" You'll get those from your boss and/or fellow salespeople. Some will be obvious; others will be specific to your product or service. While on the subject of questions, I want to mention *SPIN Selling* by Neil Rackham. This book is all about asking questions and is one of the best books I have ever read about the sales process.

Bill: What's the craziest thing that's happened in your sales career?
Eric: Nothing too crazy comes to mind for me. I've had the opportunity to meet some great people who I have learned a lot from, and I value those relationships. I've been able to enjoy some cool travel, but nothing super crazy…yet.

The second meeting.

The next step in the sales process is the second meeting. The more complex the product or service, the longer the sales cycle and the more meetings you will have. Remember, each meeting is just a conversation. Depending on what was discussed in the first meeting, you might do a technical dive in the second meeting (bringing along a technical resource to help of course!). Often there are just a couple of meetings and then a back-and-forth via email. Again, it's just a conversation between two people. It's not that tough!

At some point, either after the first meeting or the 32nd (just kidding), there will be a "Go" or "No go"—you either got the sale, or you didn't.

Sidebar: Here's a little secret, "No" just means "No today." Just because a prospect turned you down today doesn't mean it's over forever. I had dozens and dozens of sales over my career that started with the client initially saying, "No."

Bill: What's the one piece of advice you would give to someone new to sales?
Eric: What if I give you a few simple rules?
1) Focus on selling something that you believe in and you can stand behind.

2) Never burn a bridge because you never know where that person will show up again in your life.

3) Understand that sales is about pursuing opportunities and having the chance to show how your products/services can be a good fit to solve problems.

4) Winning and losing can be influenced by a ton of factors, some you control and some you don't—budget, shifting needs/priorities, timing, business value, product capability, etc.

5) Keep it all in perspective. You will win some and lose some. Reflect and learn but don't dwell. When you lose, was it because of factors that you couldn't control or was it something you did or could have done better? It doesn't have to be a personal attack or make you feel terrible if you can keep the right perspective.

6) It's all about the team. You can lose alone but you can't win alone. Be sure to celebrate the people who help you because your sales success depends on all the other departments who support you and your customer.

Let me tie everything together to end this chapter with a story. The biggest sale of my career was with a client who initially turned our product down. They had worked with another salesperson (one of the original owners), and I knew one of the reasons they didn't sign with us was the lack of timely responses to their questions.

I reached out and told them that I wanted to revisit the idea of them becoming a client and that my superpower was quick responses. It took months of meetings (this was a multi-million-dollar sale after all), but I got them signed and earned hundreds of thousands of dollars in commissions over the years from that one client. All because I did what was unexpected but needed—replying quickly and not leaving them hanging.

One final note. If you are a little uncomfortable on the conversation front consider joining a Toastmasters club (Toastmasters.org). Toastmasters' meetings provide a supportive environment to improve your public speaking, communication, and leadership skills. There are numerous clubs in almost every city. There are also online Toastmaster clubs that meet only virtually. It's an enjoyable and affordable way of gaining great communication skills!

Chapter takeaways!

- Ask questions.
- Listen.
- Take notes.
- Respond promptly.
- Have a conversation.

It's really that simple.

Chapter 4

Getting Started

---

*On the application, I actually wrote the words,
"I am the guy you are looking for"
—cocky, but it worked. I got the job.*

Claude McGee
Director of Corporate Clean Energy Solutions at Pivot Energy

If you have stuck around this far, I think it's safe to assume you might be considering a career in sales. So, let's get right to it!

With any job, the fit with your personality and temperament is very important—even more so with a career in sales because the product or service you are selling is, essentially, you!

So, how do you land that first sales job?

Meet Claude McGee

Bill: What did you want to be when you were growing up?

Claude: I wanted to be a professional surfer.

Bill: What did you do before you went into sales and what/who got you into sales?

Claude: I had three jobs. I was working as a concierge at the Moana Surfrider Hotel in Honolulu by day, waiting tables at night, and teaching English as a Second Language in what little free time I had. Even working three jobs, I still had negative cash flow at the end of the month, and I realized I had to do something different, so I got my real estate license in Hawaii. As I was building my real estate career, I saw a job advertised in the newspaper (back when jobs were advertised in the newspaper). I was down to a couple of grand in the bank and my son was a few months from being born. This job looked amazing—selling oceanfront new-construction real estate on the Big Island. I wanted the job. No, I needed the job. On the application, I actually wrote the words, "I am the guy you are looking for"—cocky, but it worked. I got the job. I call it my "step-up job"— the first time I made good money.

Sell something you love!

You don't want to sell something that doesn't excite you if you don't have to. Take an inventory of your interests. If you enjoy computers, look for a software or IT company sales position. If you are into home improvement, look into sales positions with building contracts or commercial sales with Lowes. If you enjoy decorating, maybe furniture sales is a possibility.

Once you find what you love, think a little outside the box. A love of cars doesn't necessarily mean selling Audis or Fords. It could also be auto parts or performance accessories. You could also use your previous industry experience to become a salesperson or recruiter (recruiters are salespeople!) for that field. Think about all the things your previous employer purchased, from raw materials to specialized software. Your knowledge of that industry can be a great start to selling products and services to similar companies.

> **Bill:** You enter an elevator with your dream client who asks you what you do for a living. How do you respond?
>
> **Claude:** I work with corporations to help them save money on their electricity bills while simultaneously lowering their carbon footprint. We do this by adding solar to their real estate, solar carports, and roof-mounted or ground-mounted solar arrays. We provide turnkey services, from utility bill analysis to finance to construction and all the way to interconnection with the utility company.

Sell something you understand!

Even if you don't have a passion for what a company sells, you can still make a lot of money if you understand what the product or service does, how it helps, or what problem it solves. You don't have to be an expert. Just understand it.

Be excited about it!

Whether you love the product or service you represent or simply understand how it helps others, you need to be excited about what it is you are selling. I sold radio ads for 16 years and loved everything about the radio industry. I spent the next 20 years in technology sales, focusing on software training. I didn't love the field but was excited about what companies could do with our technology, which made earning a great living possible.

Another thing to think about when deciding on what product or service you want to sell is whether you want to represent something that costs a lot (with fewer sales each year) or is less expensive (with more sales over the course of a year).

Big-ticket sales usually involve:

- Higher dollar-figure sales (sometimes in the millions).
- Sales cycles that can run months, sometimes over a year.
- Fewer sales during the course of a year.
- Lots of details, requiring more paperwork.
- Multiple decision-makers.

Examples of big-ticket sales include real estate (especially commercial leasing), medical equipment, enterprise software, or manufacturing and engineering sales. Big-ticket sales usually require multiple meetings with several different decision-makers, and you typically have to wait a considerable amount of time to know whether or not you won the sale.

Smaller-ticket sales usually involve:

- Smaller dollar-figure sales.
- Short sales cycles that run a day or a couple of weeks.
- Multiple sales during the course of a year.
- Fewer details, so less paperwork.
- Few decision-makers, often only one.

With smaller ticket sales, the decision is made relatively quickly. You will hear "No" a lot more often, but you will also hear "Yes" a great deal more!

Bill: What's the craziest thing that's happened in your sales career?

Claude: I had a condo in escrow in Hawaii, and I was representing the buyer. The seller was at the escrow office signing closing docs, he asked the escrow agent for some water, and when she turned her back, he grabbed the closing documents and ran out of the office and disappeared. My buyer was scheduled to fly from Japan to Honolulu to enjoy his new condo, and I had to call my buyer and explain the situation (in Japanese). It was crazy—after about three days, the seller resurfaced and signed the docs, so it all worked out, but it was a stressful couple of days.

Choose your selling method.

There are several methods of selling. In-person (face-to-face), over the phone (think telemarketing), virtual (video conferencing), and hybrid.

Today, virtual selling is by far the most popular method for getting sales. Either by itself or mixed with a little face-to-face (hybrid selling), virtual work is a great way to get in front of clients from around the world.

With today's technology, prospects don't have to have salespeople come to the office, and salespeople can be way more efficient with their day. Back when I sold radio ads face-to-face, I might have had three or four appointments set up for the day. I would drive across town and get stood up (ghosted in 2023 terminology). When I sold IT services, all my appointments were virtual. I might start the day meeting with a prospect in Europe, followed by appointments in the U.S. Once in a while,

I might have a client/prospect call with someone in Australia or Asia, which would be 6:00 p.m. my time.

In the end, deciding to work remotely is a personal decision.

>**Bill:** Describe your typical day.
>
>**Claude:** I wake up, drink coffee, walk up to my home office, and start working. I work 8–10-hour days, but I do have flexibility. If the surf is good, I can take a break and head out to the ocean (it is only a 10-minute drive) or go for a run. I work hard, and hours can be long, but I create my own schedule.

Research companies and industries.

Today, there are numerous ways to research industries and individual companies. You can and should still do broad searches like "medical equipment sales careers"—substitute whatever industry you are interested in. Click around company career pages and on LinkedIn. LinkedIn is the world's largest professional network on the internet. It's free and a tremendous resource for information to help find a job and research prospects once you land your job. LinkedIn profiles can be used to research companies, recruiters, hiring managers, and other influencers.

Industry associations are also great places to find information. Blog posts, webinars, white papers, and other valuable study resources exist.

Some websites also catalog valuable insights into what it's like to work at a specific company. Sites like Repvue (specific to sales) and Glassdoor are two of the better-known review sites.

Most of the major job boards (Monster, Indeed, Zip Recruiter) also have review sections. Additionally, you can search for "What's it like to work at Acme Corporation" to get different insights. One thing to note, people will bitch and complain more than they will praise, so keep an open mind when reading reviews. Like everything else, it will help if there are dozens or even hundreds of reviews for a particular company versus seven.

Finally, if you really want to get the inside scoop on a particular company, take a sales rep or manager to lunch. You can do it virtually by sending them a $20 e-gift card to a local restaurant and chatting through lunch. Most people will be flattered to be asked about their work and will talk about themselves, their company, and their career at length. I have found most companies will also share the email addresses of their salespeople. Don't be afraid to send a quick note and follow up the next day to schedule the lunch or meeting.

Ask questions like:

1. What does a typical day look like for you?
2. What are the biggest trends in your industry over the next year? Next five years?
3. What do you like and dislike about your job?
4. What advice would you give to someone considering a job in your industry?
5. What was your favorite client interaction?
6. What was your least favorite?

You will get valuable feedback and insight as well as build your network in your chosen industry! If you are currently employed, spend some time with the sales reps in your company.

Bill: How is sales different from what you were expecting? What surprised you about your current job?

Claude: I have been in sales for 25 years, so it is difficult to answer this, but at the end of the day, I think it is that so many things we do in life are sales. Getting my wife to date and then marrying me—sales. Getting my kids to eat vegetables—sales. Sales is just making your case with the customer(s) and then asking for the business. It doesn't have to be adversarial; as a matter of fact, when done right, it is not adversarial at all.

Pro tip: Don't be afraid to ask the big dogs, a heavy hitter in the industry. First, it will show you have courage and that you are not afraid to approach someone important. Second, you will be surprised how often they will respond!

Bill Bartmann was a business legend in the late 90s. His company CFS was established to purchase bad debts and similar nonproductive assets from banks and other financial institutions. It was a new industry made possible by the high rate of bank failures.

He was on the cover of Forbes Magazine, and his business was a case study at Harvard Business School. He became a multi-billionaire. It was a rare day that he or his company wasn't in the Tulsa World. Then he lost it all because of his partner.

He then became a motivational speaker. I had always wanted to meet and talk to him. His story was pretty incredible; poor, rich, broke, billionaire, broke again, and then successful for the umpteenth time. I got his email address and asked if I could buy him coffee someday. He replied almost immediately, *"What about today?"* Oh shit! Not going to lie; I was a tad intimidated but didn't have time to be that nervous. He couldn't have been more gracious, and we ended up talking longer than I had asked for.

> **Bill:** What's the one piece of advice you would give to someone new to sales?
>
> **Claude:** Block time on your calendar for yourself. Sales as a job can take over your life if you let it, the money is good but it is possible to work 24/7 because the work is never done. You owe it to yourself to give yourself some me time.

Novelist Marcia Martin had what I consider the greatest quote on life that I ever heard…"What I point out to people is that it's silly to be afraid that you're not going to get what you want if you ask. Because you are already not getting what you want. They always laugh about that because they realize it's so true. Without asking, you already have failed; you already have nothing. What are you afraid of? You're afraid of getting what you already have! It's ridiculous! Who cares if you don't get it when you ask for it because, before you ask for it, you don't have it anyway. So, there's really nothing to be afraid of."

She's right! Why would you be afraid of asking for anything in life? If you don't have something you want, you have nothing to lose by asking.

How salespeople get paid.

You probably think you know this one already, right? You sell something, you get paid. You aren't wrong, but it's a little more complex than that. Companies use a variety of different plans to compensate their salespeople. This is one of the best benefits of having a sales job! If you need or want more money, all you have to do is close more sales. Remember, sales is the one job where you can make more money than your boss!

Some sales jobs feature 100% commission. This means that your entire compensation is based on what you sell, with no guaranteed income. Sometimes employers will put a new sales rep on a salary during the training and orientation phase, but this isn't always the case. There might be months where you make tons of sales and months where you make none. A 100% commission-based pay doesn't work for everyone.

Most quality companies offer some sort of income protection for their sales reps in the form of a base salary. A base salary is a guaranteed amount of money (many IT sales positions have six-figure base salaries) and usually comes with a lower commission rate.

A draw is similar, but it goes against what you sell. Here's an example: You have a $75,000 draw against a commission rate of 10%. This means you must sell $750,000 worth of products or services before making extra money. Think of the draw as an advance against future commissions.

You typically want to look for a job with a draw or base salary.

Chapter takeaways!

- Sell something you are interested in. It doesn't have to be your passion, but it helps if it excites you.
- Look at a variety of sales jobs related to the industry you want to work in.
- Don't be afraid to talk to other salespeople. They often want to talk about their work.
- Understand the compensation structure of different industries and companies.

OK, you have figured out what you want to sell and have an idea of who you would like to sell for. Now it's time to get this dream job.

Turn the page!

Chapter 5

Land Your First Sales Job
Even if the company isn't hiring.

---

*If you want something you've never had,
you must do something you've never done.*

Dua Elayan Obeidallah

You are already a sales pro. You sold yourself when you interviewed for a job. You sold your earning power and trustworthiness when you applied for a loan. You sold when you tried to convince a friend to check out a new restaurant. You have sold your experience, education, creative thinking, and many other things throughout your life.

Landing a sales job, especially your first sales job, is different from what you are probably used to. Resumes are out. Why? You don't have any sales experience to list! I'm not saying you shouldn't have a resume handy, just that you aren't going to use it as your primary job-hunting tool.

You won't apply online because those applications go through HR, and they won't consider you because…you don't have any sales experience! I'll go one step further. In 2023, artificial intelligence has made applying for any job online useless. A bot reads your resume every time you apply. I see so many posts about people never hearing back on job applications and even getting ghosted on interviews.

As you are learning, the process of getting that first sales job is different, but in the end, it's very straightforward. In my opinion, the following method is the only way to apply for a job today.

How to get that first sales job.

You have probably heard the adage, "It's not what you know—it's who you know." Fair or not, it's even more true in sales! When looking to land that first sales job, what if you could get a referral from the owner, general manager, or president of the company you want to work for? That's another great thing about LinkedIn. Once you join and start connecting to people you already know, you might find out they know someone you want to meet!

You can and here is how!

Companies exist to make a profit. Yes, many companies also want to change the world, but you don't get to stay in business and do great things if you don't create more revenue than your monthly expenses. See the dot-com bust of 1999 or the recent crypto crash if you need any examples.

Companies go out of business for one simple reason, not enough sales. In a cold, brutal world, human assets are divided into two categories: those that produce revenue and those that only show up on the expense ledger.

Every single company executive—owner, manager, board member, etc. is very interested in talking to anyone who can help increase their revenue. As I write this, in the first quarter of 2023, there are weekly examples of companies announcing record profits yet also announcing huge layoffs.

Yeah, many of these companies are tied to Wall Street, and it is reprehensible, but that is the world we live in today.

There's a lot of copycat slashing of payroll and other expenses by private companies as well. What does all this mean? The only way to increase profits is to sell more stuff; individuals who can help will get special attention!

Meet Tony Georr

Bill: What did you want to be when you were growing up?

Tony: A cab driver because I loved to drive.

Bill: What did you do before you went into sales and what/who got you into sales?

Tony: Before sales, I was driving a cab in Tulsa. One day, I picked up a real estate broker who needed a ride to the airport at 4:00 a.m. We had a conversation on the way about real estate. When I dropped her off, I received a text from her with a broker's number. She urged me to call and promised me that it would change my life. It truly did!!!

The plan to get a referral from the boss!

When you are contacting potential employers, start at the top. Go to the owner, General Manager, Branch Manager, Regional Vice-President, etc. Write a short letter—yes, an actual letter—explaining that you are a current customer, and you feel that spending 10 minutes with you could drastically impact their bottom line in the next 12 months! Not too many people are going to ignore a bold statement like that! If you are not a current customer, buy something, even if it's a relatively insignificant purchase.

If you cannot honestly state that you are a current customer, tell them you have been talking to some of their customers and have important information to share.

> **Pro tip:** If you want to really make sure they see your pre-call note, send it in a priority mail envelope! It might be the best $10 you ever spent.

Crazy ideas to land an initial meeting!

- Go to Etsy and search 'persistent.' Purchase a small item and then send it to your contact with a note stating that when they sell items like that, they're talking about you!

- Send a plant with a note about being able to help cultivate new customers.

- Send a business management or marketing book with an inscription about developing customers being the single most important management objective. When you call, tell the receptionist you are the one who sent the book.

- Send them a menu from a restaurant with a note touting, "Today's Special is Important Information Concerning the Future of Your Company!"

These might seem silly (they are), and they might feel uncomfortable (they will be), but do something to get noticed. **You need your purple cow moment** (Google it).

Follow up your note with a phone call asking to meet with them for 10 minutes. If they are local, ask for a face-to-face meeting. If they are out of town, ask for a virtual meeting on Zoom or one of the other virtual meeting platforms. Zoom is the most popular.

You can go to Zoom.us and get the app for free. There is also a test meeting you can use to try everything out. Once you have it, spend a weekend practicing with friends and relatives. It's really easy to use, but you don't want your first time using it to be when your future is on the line! You should also go to

EventBrite.com and register for some webinars to attend. There are hundreds to choose from, and it will allow you to further practice your virtual meeting skills!

When you meet, the most important thing you can show them is confidence! Tell them about your passion for their business and how you can use that passion to create sales for them. Mention the fact that you know you don't have any sales experience, but you are sure that many of their top reps started out with little to no experience. You have already shown your creativity and determination by getting a meeting with a "top-level decision maker" (them)!

These business heads are not used to dealing with someone like you. The audacity you showed to get that 10-minute meeting will get you that referral to their sales manager or to HR. You will still be asked about your background, and this is where your story comes into play. Like every other salesperson in history, you grew up dreaming of a job, and it certainly wasn't in sales! You've spent the past 5, 10, 15–20 years doing whatever you have been doing, and you have come to the realization that a sales career offers everything you have ever wanted in a job, and it's the path to a better life for you and your family.

Sample dialogue.

Here is some sample dialogue to use (use your own words) about why you are looking to get into sales at this point in your life.

Decision Maker (Pat) – "Jamie, why are you interested in sales?"

Jamie – "Pat, I am excited (much better than 'interested') about a career in sales because the skills that are required to be successful are the same skills I've used throughout my life."

"I talked to several salespeople in this industry, including a couple with your company (your earlier research shows your passion and preparation). My love of 'X' (X being the product or service) and my desire to control my own destiny led me to the only career option that would satisfy those needs—sales!

"In terms of skills, I feel the most important are persistence and tenacity, an ability to relate to people, and problem-solving. Those skills have marked my life since high school." (They are looking for patterns of behavior, which is why it's imperative you go back over your life up to this point.) "In high school, I wanted to be a starter on the basketball team even though I never played competitively during the summers like a lot of kids. I practiced on my own throughout the summer before my sophomore year and barely made the team. I continued looking for small ways to improve my game, focused on the stuff most players overlooked, and eventually concentrated on rebounding. I played a lot of pickup games with local college players the summer before my senior year and became a starter halfway through the season.

"Two years ago, I headed up a project to help a local homeless shelter find a new location. It was a challenge because no one wanted it near them (here is where your problem-solving skills come into play). We constantly had to fight the not-in-my-backyard feeling. We found an old building that had been closed for years and pushed through the necessary permits in record time. We literally sat in the City Hall offices to expedite the process. Then we went out and got the necessary supplies and materials needed to make the building ready. We did it through a series of donations from the public, fundraising from a couple of local charities, and finding unused items within our own homes and the homes of family and friends. We also set up some minor work assignments for some of the shelter clients in exchange for funds for ongoing expenses like utilities.

"I am excited about a sales career because, after 10 years as a front-line supervisor, I know this is the right career move for my family and me.

No one grows up wanting to be a salesperson—you know this as well as I do—but I realize this job gives me the opportunity to take care of my family and have true job satisfaction. This is where I need to be."

There was no discussion about previous sales experience. Instead, Jamie pointed out what they felt were the attributes of a successful salesperson and highlighted those attributes with their own personal experience. They were highlighting their life skills that are transferable to a sales career. Remember, you are not asking for a job; you are asking for the opportunity to rebuild your life by selling their products or services.

Pro tip: As soon as the interview is over, write a thank you note and mail it! Do not send an email. Thank you notes are powerful because very few people send them anymore.

For several years, I taught prisoners a workshop at the Tulsa County Jail about why they should seriously consider sales when released. I read about prison schools in the paper and thought if there was ever a group of individuals who could use my message, these men and women were it.

I could always count on a couple of things happening at

each session. First, someone would make the joke, "Hey, sales is what got me in here!" That always got a laugh, but later on, someone in a more serious tone would ask, "How am I going to get hired with my criminal record?" When I said I had an answer, the room would get quiet.

I would tell them about the pre-call letter and how to follow it up. Once they were in front of the decision-maker, they needed to have their come-to-Jesus moment and bear their soul. I told them they would have to admit to their past mistakes and explain that they know how important a good job is to help rebuild their lives.

Most importantly, they must humanize their message by owning up to their past and their desire to improve their lives and the lives of their loved ones by selling the hell out of this particular product or service.

They need to say out loud that they know a lot of people would not give them a second chance, but if they got this sales job, they would excel with this opportunity.

Look, you don't need six or eight jobs. You just need one job. A job with a company run by someone who understands that this particular individual sitting in front of them (or on their computer screen) is an absolute gift! You just need one person to understand that you would be more motivated to succeed in selling their company than probably any of their current salespeople.

I shared these examples to show that everyone, regardless of background and circumstances, can come up with a compelling story to create a job offer from scratch.

My examples!

Let me share a couple of examples of how I handled getting an interview.

Example #1: After I decided that the pay for being a radio DJ wasn't what I wanted, I decided to go after a job selling radio ads. I put in an application every few months but nothing; nada, diddly squat. I decided I needed to get the attention of the general manager. I sent a short letter stating that I wanted to talk to him about a sales job, and if he didn't hire me, he could keep the enclosed check for $250. This was 1980 when $250 wasn't chump change.

> **Sidebar:** I didn't have that in my account at the time.

I got the meeting and sold myself. I said, "Give me all the crap accounts no one wants and a goal to hit in six months. If I don't hit the goal, I'll throw myself out." I got the job (and the check back…whew!). He also took me up on my offer to take all the crap accounts, including quite a few businesses that had been blown away by a historic tornado in the adjoining town earlier in the year (actually, it was seven tornados; Google "Night of the Twisters"). I loved being inside the operations of the radio station. I grew up listening to and learned some of my earliest lessons on sales success—including how your coworkers (in this case, copywriters) could really help you close a sale. After a couple of years at the station, I left to start a video rental store, which was fun until Blockbuster came along.

Example #2: This was my last radio sales job before I went into IT sales. I saw an ad for a salesperson at a radio station in Tulsa and dropped off my resume and cover letter in person. The next day I called to follow up. Only one problem. The ad said, "No phone calls." I can still remember the sigh the sales manager let out when he picked up the phone and I told him I was following up on my cover letter and resume. He then said, "The ad said no calls." I told him I understood but was doing whatever it took to get the job and would use the same passion and persistence to sell his radio station. I got the job. Now, that totally could have backfired on me. He could have ripped me for not following directions, but it was a calculated risk. Remember the quote from Marcia Martin. I already didn't have the job, so the worst thing that could happen was I still didn't have the job.

My approach to getting a sales job and landing clients was always the same. I was different than most (like returning calls and emails immediately).

It reminds me of a great quote from former football coach Steve Spurrier:

"There are two ways of doing things. You can do it the way everyone else does, which means you got to do it much better than them, or you can do it differently. So, you want to be better; why don't you try to be a little different?"

The two things you must show in the pursuit of your first sales job are:

- **Persistence!** Keep after your contact until you get the interview. Follow up if you don't get hired immediately after the meeting. Persistence can overcome a lot. You should point out that the energy you are using to get hired is the same energy you'll use to close sales.
- **Passion!** Talk about your love of what their company does and how representing their products or services will help change your life. Make the conversation about your future and how you figure your success is tied to theirs.

Bill: What's the craziest thing that's happened in your sales career?

Tony: One time, the buyer met me at a final walkthrough 45 minutes prior to closing and never showed up to the closing! Two weeks later, he emailed me apologizing that he freaked out and couldn't do it!

A point about money and motivation.

All successful salespeople are motivated by money to some degree. I told one of my last bosses that the whole key-to-fame-and-fortune thing was a myth. It's always about the fortune. (At least it was for me.)

Anyone hiring salespeople wants to hear that making money motivates their sales candidates. You should allude to this during your interview when you are talking about what the sales job can do for you. I only bring this up if the situation dictates that you say this part out loud.

During the interview, tell them you are tired of someone else dictating how much money you earn. You are equally fed up with your annual earnings tied to things outside your control. Humanizing your desire to make more money is a powerful way to convince someone to hire you. Your personal motivation and drive mean you will require less time from management to motivate you to sell.

Questioning the questioner.

You know the basics of your message when you meet with the decision-maker. Hopefully, you've practiced it numerous times. At some point, you will probably get to ask your own questions. In your case, questions will serve two purposes. First, to gain information, and second, to show how smart you are and help to gain the trust of the person you are questioning. Let's take a look.

1. **How do you help new salespeople grow professionally?** This will give you insight into how they onboard new salespeople and the training and support they give to newbies.

2. **Do you encourage system selling or out-of-the-box thinking?** This can be kind of tricky. As a brand-new salesperson, it can't hurt to follow an established process, but, at the same time, think about what Steve Spurrier said about being different. Hopefully, it's a company that is open to both approaches.

3. **Do you manage results or activity for new salespeople?** This can be a gray area as well. Obviously, results are what matters for both you and the company. Activity will be important in the beginning as they will want to see you talk to prospects, but activity for activity's sake is counterproductive. If you are expected to talk to X number of prospects each week without regard to their quality, that's a red flag.

Bill: What's the one piece of advice you would give to someone new to sales?

Tony: I have two pieces of advice:

1. Sales is a numbers game. If you make your calls and follow up today, you'll sell tomorrow. In my

personal experience as a realtor, this is what I have found:

    a.   100 calls > 30 conversations > 10 appointments > 2-4 transactions.

2.   Be honest. Don't be afraid to bust a million-dollar deal if it's not in your client's best interest. Answer your phone and stay in touch even after the sale is complete. Your integrity will serve you well.

Chapter takeaways!

- Successful salespeople are persistent and use their passion to get creative in their hunt for sales. You must bring those same characteristics to the table to land your first sales job.
- It's about who you know, so get to know the people who circulate your chosen industry.
- Ask questions and listen.
- And one final note from Tony Georr—I would've said good luck but it's not luck...it's simply hard work.

Chapter 6

You Got the Job, Now What

In the end, sales will not only make you money but teach you so much more about yourself than you ever knew.

Travis Shelton
Senior Account Executive at Instawork

Congratulations! You got hired, and your start date is fast approaching. What the hell do you do now? Like all good salespeople, you prepare.

You already studied your new company and its industry when you were preparing for your interview. Now it's time to go full Ph.D. and learn as much as possible before your first day!

You will get product training when you start. I'm talking about immersing yourself in the industry and your new company.

Meet Travis Shelton

Bill: What did you want to be when you were growing up?

Travis: Growing up in the lower middle class, I had dreams of becoming an astronaut. Looking up at the stars and realizing there is so much more beyond Earth fascinated me at such a young age. You learn quickly at a young age that dreams and reality are so far apart.

Bill: What did you do before you went into sales and what/who got you into sales?

Travis: Prior to sales, I spent eight years serving in the United States Marines as a Staff Sergeant. My eight years were split—four years in Kaneohe Bay, HI, and four years in West Lafayette, IN. I spent eight months on a tour in Southern Helmand,

Afghanistan, where you realize very quickly all the things to appreciate and be grateful for. Once I transitioned and prior to graduating from Purdue University, I was approached by a recruiter for sales. I didn't really know what to expect or what I was getting into but the idea of creating your own wealth by your effort was exciting.

Pro Tip! Ask for the paperwork before your first day. Get that nonsense out of the way so you will be able to focus on the important stuff. Everyone knows salespeople hate paperwork!

To do this, visit your company's website and read press releases and blog posts. Keep an eye out for case studies. They are a great education and show you exactly how customers successfully use your product or service.

Spend a lot of time on LinkedIn! Look for industry groups to join. Follow people within your company as well as industry leaders. Following colleagues allows you to see what they write about and comment on your LinkedIn feed. You can even enable a notification every time they do something. It's a great way to stay on top of things! Once you identify these industry leaders, see if they list any active social media accounts. If so, consider following them there as well.

Once you find interesting people and groups to follow, comment on their posts. That's a great way to get visibility. Others will see your comments and check out your profile. Building visibility in these groups will help you connect with your community, and sales is all about connections.

Next, you should Google, "industry name," and "trends." You'll get some great resources to check out. For example, I searched "medical scanning" and "trends" and got these results:

Definitive Healthcare
https://www.definitivehc.com › blog › future-trends-in... ⋮
4 Trends in Medical Imaging Changing Healthcare
Medical imaging market trends · **Artificial intelligence (AI)** · Augmented intelligence · Virtual and augmented reality & 3D medical imaging · Nuclear imaging.

AQ Modern Diagnostic Imaging
https://aqmdi.com › 5-medical-technology-and-imagin... ⋮
5 Medical Imaging Trends that are Changing Healthcare
5 emerging **medical** technology and **imaging trends** that have brought revolutionary changes in the healthcare industry by improving diagnostic **imaging**.

This will help you understand what is happening in the industry and increase your comfort with the lingo.

Another thing to note is that when doing a search, Google will suggest other questions that you might find helpful:

If you click on those dropdown arrows on the right, you will get detailed answers to each of those questions.

Go to YouTube and search for speeches and presentations from people with your company and industry leaders. Seeing and hearing the information will hit differently than just reading everything. Plus, you will find videos of product presentations. If you are a podcast fan, search for interesting podcasts from industry leaders.

This is also a good time to check out your competitors. Go to their website and read their blog posts and press releases. Sign up for their newsletter.

Read! Find books written by industry experts. Ensure they aren't too old; trends in most fields change too fast to read something from even five years ago. Extensive studying will serve you well.

Now teach somebody! I am assuming you are taking great notes with all this research because you are going to use it to teach someone about your company and industry!

One of the best ways to learn about anything is to teach it to someone else.

So, pick out your significant other, best friend, or random stranger at the grocery store and do a book report on your new company and/or industry. You could use your dog, but you want follow-up questions. FYI, if your dog is able to pose follow-up questions, you don't need a sales career…you need an agent!

> **Bill:** You enter an elevator with your dream client who asks you what you do for a living. How do you respond?
>
> **Travis:** I help people. I provide an app-based labor platform to my clients that allows them to create agility around their labor needs and reduce overall labor costs. At the same time, I provide professionals with an opportunity to provide for their families in a flexible way that allows for a better work-life balance.

Your first 90 days.

Regardless of whether your first day is in an actual office or attended virtually, there are some things to think about that will help ensure your success. As you take everything in, think about developing a 90-day plan of action.

This is where your pre-start research comes in. You should have a decent handle on the product/service you will be selling and have questions that popped up during that research. You want to ask your boss and several other salespeople those questions. Having different perspectives will be tremendously helpful and allow you to create your own.

Ask to see as many demonstrations as possible during these first few weeks. One of the advantages of working virtually is it's easier to record all your meetings for replay. If your meeting software doesn't automatically transcribe the conversations, you can upload the video to YouTube, where it is done automatically—be sure to ask permission before and make the video private.

Bill: How is sales different from what you were expecting? What surprised you about your current job?

Travis: The general idea of sales sounds easier from the verbiage compared to the day-to-day expectations. My first sales job was face-to-face commission-only sales. They tell you if you just talk to enough people, you'll make sales and the rest will follow. The average KPI was to talk to 150 people and get maybe 15 to stop. Out of the 15 who stop, you pitch 10, of those 10, you close two per day. It was intense and each day was about 10–12 hours—or until you got the sales you needed. If you didn't make a sale, then you knew you were going home with no money for your work and effort that day. That was the moment I realized sales was a grind, and you had to have grit in order to make it in this business. In my current role, it's a change of pace. I am a Senior Account Executive now for a tech startup. I enjoy what I do in my sales career now. The grind is still there but I'm a part of a small group responsible for the growth of our company and launching new markets each quarter. I'm surprised every day that my job has so much purpose and meaning behind it compared to prior sales roles.

Learn the lingo. Every industry has its own terminology. You probably came across terms you didn't understand during your pre-start research. Now is the time to ask what the hell is a 'Mass Bit Manipulator' (Google it)!

Start reaching out to your fellow salespeople in the company and introduce yourself. You might be assigned a mentor, which is great, but you want to get as many perspectives as possible from as many salespeople as possible.

Ask to sit in on a meeting with different salespeople in the next couple of weeks.

Your coworkers are vital to your success. I devoted a whole chapter about it later in the book. Ask them about the hardest sale they ever made. Most salespeople like to share victories; this will be an excellent opportunity to learn from actual events and how they handled challenges.

Ask them if they would share a typical prospecting email they use. Marketing will undoubtedly have some templates for you, but the most effective cold-call emails are short and to the point, not dressed up in HTML code to make it look all cute and fancy. Ask them what their favorite questions are for new prospects.

Bill: Describe your typical day.

Travis: The majority of my days, I have full autonomy. A typical day consists of day prep from 7:30-9:00 a.m., followed by a call block from 9:00-10:30 a.m. From 10:30 a.m. to 3:00 p.m., I schedule new client meetings/demos. There is a mix of internal meetings in there as well. From 3-5:00 p.m., I run another call block. Having meetings is great but at the same time, I have to protect my call blocks to make sure meetings don't dry out. In the launch markets, we have 90 days to create as much economic growth as possible before handing off those markets to new reps to continue growing them while we head into brand-new ones.

Talk to your company's support system! Does your company have a Help Desk? Is there a parts or service department? Ask them what they wish the salespeople knew. Typically, these workers are the face of the company after you close the sale. They know the common problems, complaints, and issues that come up. Keep in mind, "A complaint is a demand for a solution to a problem." Your support teams are a goldmine of information; most will be pleased that someone asks for their opinion.

Spoiler alert! You will suck the first few times you do a sales demo. Everyone does. You might even have all the knowledge down perfectly, but nerves will interfere at some point.

You need to practice. Start out demonstrating to yourself, then friends and family. Your dog might have some killer follow-up questions to offer!

You should also practice your appointment call. I know what you are thinking, "What the hell Bill! You said cold calling is dead back in Chapter 2!" I did, and it is, but you aren't cold calling. You are following up on an email or LinkedIn message you sent.

Believe it or not, it's actually better if they don't answer! This allows you to leave a message referencing your previous email or social media message, leading them to go read it. I've used this technique successfully over the years. There's less tension between you and the prospect (because they didn't answer their phone and found a salesperson on the other end), and it encourages them to read your finely crafted email.

Don't be afraid to ask any questions that pop into your head. You're new; you are not supposed to know much in the beginning. Also, don't be afraid to say, "I don't know." This is super important with customers and prospects. Don't try to bullshit your way through something to which you don't have the answer. Simply tell them you don't know, but you will have the answer before the end of the day. Then get the answer! If something prevents you from answering that day, be honest in your follow-up call.

Contacts are your most important asset. They are the lifeblood of every salesperson. Email addresses and phone numbers for both prospects (people who have yet to buy) and current customers are your contact list. These contacts become your annuity. Those who have bought from you already are very likely to buy from you again or recommend you to others. Those who haven't yet bought could do so tomorrow. Remember, "No" just means "Not today." Managing your email list is how you will communicate with everyone and build your business. Company newsletters, special offers, the latest case study, and a post from LinkedIn you think they'd be interested in reading are all opportunities to keep your name in front of the people who buy from you.

> **Bill:** What's the one piece of advice you would give to someone new to sales?
>
> **Travis:** Sales is a grind and organization. Learning the pitch and how to overcome objections can be taught. It can be developed. But a lack of organization can negate all of it. The most successful sales reps I've come across are not necessarily phenomenal salespeople or do anything over the top. They are organized and are incredible at developing their pipeline and efficiency behind follow-ups and closing clients. If you are new to sales, find your organization and find your why. Buckle up and be prepared to put in the work.

Prospecting!

This book was never designed to be a how-to book, but I wanted to share some thoughts and ideas on prospecting because it's so important to new salespeople. **Prospecting is finding more people to talk to about your product or service.** The more people you talk to, the more money you make. I did the math, and it checks out!

Being a newbie is a great opportunity to go through old records of customers who purchased years ago from salespeople who no longer work with your company. Companies often call these orphan accounts, and there are two great reasons to chase these down.

First, you might land a sale! The easiest place to find revenue is with someone who has already bought from your company. The more experienced salespeople often overlook orphan accounts because they may not be worth their time. But as a new salesperson, they are absolutely worth yours.

Second, you'll get more reps (remember the sports analogy earlier?). You need to practice talking to people, and a small current customer is a low risk and a wonderful way to build muscle memory for your talking points.

Once you've gained some experience and confidence, talk to your boss. Ask them for the names of the most difficult prospects they have. Who is the account no one else wants to deal with? In my experience, if you land someone like this, they are typically loyal as hell because they respect the sales rep who answered all their questions and fought through their bullshit.

Years ago, when I started an in-room video service that ran on the TV in hotel rooms in Texas, I came across a hotel general manager who was a piece of work. He was borderline evil. It became a matter of pride to land this guy. I eventually did, and he became a tremendous resource for me as we expanded into new cities. I don't think anyone had stood up to him before, and he respected me for it.

Chapter takeaways!

- Congrats!
- Stay up on the trends in your industry.
- Learn about your company's competitors.
- Sales is just having conversations.
- Ask questions.
- Practice your pitch. Not to memorize it, but to have the main points easily come to mind.
- A complaint is a demand for a solution to a problem.

Chapter 7

Selling Your Coworkers
(It's the secret sauce!)

---

*When I say I sold a million dollars,
I mean, we sold a million dollars.*

Bill Becker
Sales God

Hey, it's my book. I can quote myself!

As a salesperson, you will spend a lot of time working on your own. However, coworkers are vital to your success. Steve Jobs knew it as well when he spoke with '60 Minutes' in 2003 when he said, "Great things in business are never done by one person; they're done by a team of people."

Can you succeed without cultivating your coworkers? Sure, but working closely with them and fostering relationships will greatly multiply your efforts and make you more money. And while I generally try not to be an ass, I don't always succeed. But I learned early on in my sales career that going the extra mile when dealing with coworkers will lead to greater success. Much greater!

Meet Bill Becker

Bill asks: What did you want to be when you were growing up?

Bill answers: A veterinarian. I sent off for a brochure to Iowa State and then found out I had to take all these biology and chemistry classes. Um, no.

Bill asks: What did you do before you went into sales and what/who got you into sales?

Bill answers: I worked for several years at the local grocery store. Loved it! Ultimately, I wanted to be in the radio business, and after discovering that being a disk jockey didn't pay well, I jumped into radio sales.

The past few years have seen a dynamic shift in the workplace, especially with the rise of remote work. People feel less connected to their company and their coworkers than ever before.

Praising your coworkers goes beyond being a good human being. There are drugs involved! When a person receives praise or a compliment, it starts a chemical chain reaction. The brain's hypothalamus (don't worry...I had to look it up too) is triggered and begins to produce dopamine.

When I was working on the final part of onboarding a new client, there was always paperwork that needed to be filled out by my accounting department (W9s, Security Questionnaires, etc.). Since I was always friendly with those team members, I usually didn't have to wait long to get stuff filled out and returned.

I invested in my relationships with my coworkers, and it continually paid off. As a weapons-grade smartass, I always sought ways to joke around with everyone. It doesn't take much to brighten someone's day. People love to be acknowledged, even if it takes the form of good-natured ribbing.

We also had an internal Kudos Channel where everyone could give props and highlight something a particular employee did recently. I always had my special take on Kudos. First, I would head to Google Translate and enter in 'kudos' and some obscure language like Maltese.

Then I would title the post, *Awguri for Paul.* I wrote about the great thing Paul did and how it impacted the company. Many times, my posts were grandiose, so in the end, each kudos accomplished three things:

1. They were educational (readers learned a new language each time).
2. They were informative (readers learned about what their coworker did).
3. They were humorous (my smartass spin).

Bill asks: You enter an elevator with your dream client, who asks you what you do for a living. How do you respond?

Bill answers: Well, now I tell them I'm retired and that they should have met me a year ago, and I would have changed their life! Seriously though, when I was working, I'd tell them that I specialize in helping software companies create and deliver incredible hands-on training for their customers and partners.

Pro tip: Thank you notes are vital to your success. Notice I said notes and not emails. I already mentioned using them after your interview, and you'll obviously want to send one after you sign a new customer or get a referral. However, did you know that thank you notes are just as important to your internal customer, i.e., coworkers? Because no one sends them anymore!

You can get a box of 50 blank cards for less than $10 at Walmart or Amazon. If you are working in an office, it's easy peasy! Just write a simple thank you note and place it on their desk or in their cube. I cannot tell you the number of times I would see my thank you note pinned up in a cube or office. Two, three, or four sentences of appreciation will greatly impact your relationship with your coworkers. (Make sure the note is a personal compliment and not something you just made up in order to be nice.)

Bill asks: How is sales different from what you were expecting? What surprised you about your current job?

Bill answers: I just thought that sales were exactly how it was portrayed in the movies and on TV. That it was fast-talking folks pressuring people into buying something. The surprise was that, actually, sales was nothing like that. In my case, my first job selling radio ads was about creating a message to help the customers sell more of their product or service.

Share the wealth!

Typically, salespeople are the highest-paid people in a company, so it doesn't hurt to share the wealth once in a while. My favorite currency was Amazon gift cards. You can choose any amount and deliver them immediately via email or text. After you sign a client, consider tipping the coworkers who were instrumental in helping land them.

Share in good times and bad. One of the secrets to sales (and life in general) is the impact a person can make during bad times. It's easy to be happy and do the right thing when stuff is going right; it's a whole other story when things go wrong.

When problems came up at our company, it was usually the Help Desk and the sales engineers. The Help Desk is like Lost Luggage at the airport—the place where no one is in a good mood when they call. It's a tough gig and often a thankless job, especially if the customer is being a jerk. The sales engineers also dealt with angry customers. If I had a customer or prospect with an issue and someone from the Help Desk went above and beyond to help, I'd shoot them a $25 gift card. If a sales engineer overcame a difficult issue in record time, I made sure to reward them just as quickly.

Another time, right after I signed a significant client, we found out they had a major event planned two months away (normally, planning takes six months). We wanted to make sure this happened, and many people, including executives, were pulled in to make it happen. I made sure to tip everyone. The purpose was to show my appreciation to everyone, including the big bosses. It created a lot of goodwill for the rest of my career, especially when I would bring my own problems or opportunities that were out of the norm.

You can also make insignificant gestures that can make a great impact. A simple $10 Starbucks card or offer to pay off someone's speeding tickets (eh…that might not be insignificant) can go a long way. I got hurt one time, and it initially looked pretty bad. A coworker sent me cases of Pop-Tarts, and I was forever indebted to her!

Bill asks: Describe your typical day.

Bill answers: My day always started with checking email. Since I had customers all over the world, I would have messages from European clients and customers in Asia that were several hours old. I would then have a combination of meetings; some were monthly meetings with current clients and others were new prospect meetings where I would do a demo (if it was an initial meeting) or answer questions if we were meeting for the second or third time. As the day progressed, there would be new emails and requests from both clients and coworkers.

That's why I loved working from home. I could start at 6:30 a.m., work for a while, and then hit my home gym or walk my dog. Wash and repeat throughout the day.

I also periodically showed my support in a way that had nothing to do with money or gift cards. I would go to bat for a coworker if a customer or prospect was being rough on one of my fellow employees. There was a client who continually abused our Help Desk. I put her on notice that I was thinking about firing her as a customer.

She was so incensed that she hunted down the contact info for our CEO and went on and on about how I was the anti-Christ and that they would dump us if I weren't fired. The CEO rang me up and asked what was going on, and I gave him the scoop. I explained that I hated bullies, and this client was being a bully. He supported me, and the client soon left. This had an impact on my bottom line, but I would do it again. No one gets to be a chronic jerk and get away with it.

Always apologize.

Spoiler Alert! You're going to make mistakes. Everyone does, not just newbies. I made two in my last year at my job. Actually, I only made one mistake that year; the other was where

I thought I was wrong but wasn't, so technically, that was the mistake...but I digress. When you make a mistake, own up to it and apologize. Trying to deny you screwed up just makes you look bad. People know everyone makes mistakes; how you act afterward is the difference between being respected or being considered a tool everyone hates.

Here's a great example of how apologizing paid off in another career setting.

Even the casual sports fan probably has an idea who Stephen A. Smith is. He's the loud, opinionated (some say blowhard!) personality who is the highest-paid person at ESPN. Most people don't know this; it's SAS's second go-around at ESPN. He first worked there from 2009 to 2012, then he was let go because he was kind of an ass. When given the chance to return three years later, he sat in his room and wrote down the names of everyone he might have offended at the network.

He included a section about why he did what he did and even wrote out exactly how he planned to make it up to them. "I said, 'I'm going to correct the error of my ways, and I'm going to come back better than ever, and I'm going to be number one," Smith said on Good Morning America. SAS currently makes $15 million annually, so his apology tour paid off enormously!

Bill asks: What's the craziest thing that's happened in your sales career?

Bill answers: What a perfect question, Bill. Early on in the job I just retired from, I had one of my first solo meetings with a new prospect. I was nervous as hell! The meeting (virtual) started off fine with the normal introductions and pleasantries. Then I had computer issues. I couldn't hear them; they couldn't hear me. I freaked out and got upset, and I am pretty sure I invented three new cuss words, but there was only one problem. They could hear me! It was my headset. I was aghast and so embarrassed. Luckily, they were good-natured about it and said those technical challenges happen to everyone.

I share these examples so you will be on the lookout for ways to reward and acknowledge your coworkers. **We spend more of our waking hours with our coworkers than with our family.** Telling them that you respect their work and appreciate what they do is a no-brainer.

When I retired at the end of November 2022, I shared a long goodbye message with my company and my coworkers. I talked about how my job allowed me to rebuild my life and do so many great things for others. I also told them it wasn't just me but a team effort. Then I called out dozens of them and mentioned a special moment I remembered about our time together. These moments changed my life, so why not tell the people who played a part in it and let them know what they mean to me.

> **Bill asks:** What's the one piece of advice you would give to someone new to sales?
>
> **Bill answers:** Don't overcomplicate this job. There's nothing magical about sales. It literally is having conversations and helping someone decide whether or not your product or service is right for them. As you gain experience and confidence, that confidence will naturally come out and help you close even more sales.

Ultimately, being a decent human goes a long way and will be rewarding in a number of ways.

Chapter takeaways!

- Take care of your co-workers! You can't do your job successfully without them. Developing those relationships will benefit you forever.

- Showing appreciation doesn't have to cost money.
- Always apologize. No excuses.
- Be a decent human being.

Chapter 8

How to Blow Up Your Sales Career

Why do I do this?
Because the money's good,
the scenery changes,
and they let me use explosives, okay?

Steve Buscemi
from the movie *Armageddon*

Now you know why you should consider a sales career and how to research potential employers. You have also learned strategies to land your first sales job and gained insights from a wide range of current salespeople from different fields. You have your first job and are ready to hit the ground running.

But wait, there's more!

At this point, this shiny new job in this fancy new field is yours to derail. Now, most people don't make a conscious effort to derail their jobs. It usually happens because of ignorance. So, to combat that, it's time to learn some sure-fire ways to royally screw up your chances of developing into a top-notch salesperson. Avoiding these scenarios and using the skill sets that made you who you were before sales will help ensure your sales career gets off to a great start.

Watch out for these potential pitfalls.

Don't forget that buying is an emotional process!

Yes, your product or service needs to fill a need like fixing a problem or creating an opportunity for the prospect. But what buyers are really looking for is peace of mind, especially if you sell a high-dollar item. That's where great salespeople separate themselves from average ones. Prospects want to know that you will take care of them. They want to know that they made a good decision when they bought what you sold them. Everyone understands there will be bumps in the road, and prospects want to feel at ease that you will handle whatever pops up.

Meet Jeena Stanford

Bill: What did you want to be when you were growing up?

Jeena: An archaeologist.

Bill: What did you do before you went into sales and what/who got you into sales?

Jeena: I practiced as a Registered Nurse for almost 14 years. I started looking at medical device companies, EMR (EPIC/Cerner), etc. where I felt my nursing background would be a good fit, but also a company that would be willing to hire me with zero sales experience. For my first sales job, I was recruited by a home infusion pharmacy. Being an RN and former case manager, it was a natural fit and made the move into sales a pretty smooth transition. I was immediately sold and knew I wanted to remain in sales. However, I really wanted to get into healthcare technology. Most of those sales positions are only given to people who have a technical background or solid enterprise sales experience (I had neither of those). My husband was working for Lawson/Infor at the time, and they were hiring Solution Consultants to demo the Human Capital Management software within the Healthcare vertical. Although this was pre-sales vs sales, I jumped at the opportunity to get my foot in the healthcare technology space. The move was a pivotal moment in my sales career, and I'm forever thankful for the opportunity!

You take rejection personally.

Here's the thing, you are going to hear "No" a lot more than you will hear "Yes." It might not be a literal "No." It could be a "not interested," "not at this time," "next quarter or next year," or whatever. You can't take it personally!

Failure like this isn't limited to sales. "No" just means not right now. I can't tell you the number of times someone said "No" to me and later returned to buy.

You fail to become a student of your craft.

Too many people have torpedoed their sales career because they didn't continue studying the sales process. Whether you are a newbie or a 20-year veteran, you can always make tweaks to ensure success. Make a point of finding new ways to sell, whether it's a new prospecting source or coming up with a customer service idea or question you can use to uncover a new opportunity. You never graduate from the school of sales.

Bill: How is sales different from what you were expecting? What surprised you about your current job?

Jeena: I remember thinking, "Sales has to be so easy," and that I could do it based on my clinical background alone. I figured that if I can save the lives of micro-preemies weighing less than 2 lbs, I can sell anything. While in my Solution Consultant role at Infor, my sales supervisor said, "You're going to soon realize it's a different kind of stress. At the end of the day, you didn't lose a patient. However, you'll have the stress of "Did I prepare enough? Did I include the right people? Did I see the land mine our competitor planted?" Sales is a beautiful orchestration of planning, relationships, learning from your own wins and losses, etc., and I think that was the most surprising thing about my current job.

You fail to manage your time!

The only inventory you have is your time. It is pretty simple. You will fail if you do not plan your activities and organize your time.

Sidebar: Poor time management is a habit of wasting time and not completing tasks. You can spend an entire day working—organizing your files, looking through leads but never calling any, chatting with coworkers or friends until quitting time—and never actually getting anything done. You must make calls, send emails, study, and connect.

Bill: Describe your typical day.

Jeena: Some people might say they wake up and exercise or meditate, but I just want to get right to work. I'm excited about the opportunities I'm working on and the potential I haven't tapped into yet. For me, my typical day includes reprioritizing my to-do list, focusing on current opportunities, allowing time for prospecting, and making sure I'm current on any recent news within healthcare that might have an impact on my accounts.

You fail to prospect.

Prospecting is your entire job in the beginning. Chances are you won't be given any accounts when you start; if you are, they will be small accounts to give you experience, "reps" in sports terms. Your future depends on finding new prospects.

Remember when I told you to ask for the hard-to-crack-pain-in-the-ass prospects? That's a great source of leads. So are Google, LinkedIn, and social media groups that focus on your industry. **If you sell locally, but your company is national, create a peer group of salespeople from your company.** An idea or lead in Denver will probably work in San Diego. I did this to great effect in both my radio sales career and when I sold training early in my IT career. Finally, go to your competitor's website and see which customers they are bragging about. Look for a list of logos, case studies, testimonials, etc. I loved poaching new customers from my competition.

You fail to match your product or service to the prospect's needs.

Simply put, you don't listen. Remember, selling is not about persuading; it's about finding a need and helping someone fill it. All of that happens in a conversation! You'll learn early on what questions to ask prospects. Practice them.

Bill: What's the craziest thing that's happened in your sales career?

Jeena: Hitting my number and making President's Club my first year in sales. (That's more of a proud thing vs the craziest thing.) However, it isn't typical for someone new to sales to accomplish both in year one, especially considering you are focused on building a funnel, getting to know your accounts and territory, and understanding what it is you sell.

You don't say "No" enough!

I could have included this one earlier in the book, but this "No" is about setting future expectations and managing relationships. You need to learn when to say "No." Say "No" to unreasonable requests from coworkers or prospects. Just like replying quickly to a phone message or email sets the stage for people to know you will respond in a timely manner, saying "No" to unrealistic requests will let them know your time is valuable, and both sides should focus on what is important. Setting boundaries early on in the sales process will also save you big-time headaches down the road because you didn't set the precedent of agreeing to some senseless request.

You listen to your coworkers!

Wait—what!?! I know you are thinking, "Bill, didn't you say to ask your coworkers lots of questions and learn from them? You literally just told me a couple of paragraphs ago to form a peer group!" I did, and I'm glad you paid attention. Now, I am telling you to stay clear of certain coworkers. The ones who are not successful and always have an excuse. They seem to have every problem, difficulty, and reason why things cannot be sold. It's human nature to complain if nothing is going right. Watch out for these malcontents.

Bill: What's the one piece of advice you would give to someone new to sales?

Jeena: Under no circumstances should you think

you know everything. You don't. And my advice would be to take advantage of and embrace the resources available to you. It may be in the form of co-workers being a mentor to you, books, etc. Everyone learns in different ways, but I strongly feel you can't beat the experience of someone taking you under their wing and sharing years of wins and losses with you. Never turn down a conversation with a stranger (airport, grocery store, coffee shop) because you never know who is sitting next to you.

You are afraid to fail!

You don't send that email (they're free, and there's no reason not to). You don't pick up the phone (in the early days of my career, I used to hope for voicemail, so I could leave a message and not worry about screwing up live).

Your stomach is in knots before your Zoom meeting starts with a prospect (been there, done that, seen the movie, and read the book). All of it is normal!

We all have a tendency to overthink everything. We waste a ton of time and energy thinking and rethinking. Eventually, you have to trust yourself and make a decision! Even if it's the wrong decision.

Stop thinking and pick up the phone or hit 'send' on that email.

Author Sylvester McNutt III said it better than I ever could. "Overthinking is the biggest waste of human energy. Trust yourself, make a decision, and gain more experience. There is no such thing as perfect. You cannot think your way into perfection; just take action."

> **Bill:** You enter an elevator with your dream client who asks you what you do for a living. How do you respond?
>
> **Jeena:** If things go as planned, you'll soon find out. But seriously: I am a provider of "XYZ" product, and it's my job to make your life easier. Do you have five minutes to chat? Depending on what the product is or the role of the person in the elevator, the message would change a bit to point out a specific use case, benefit, etc., for the company and/or role the person is in.

You fail to commit.

This is key, maybe the most important point to remember if you go after a sales career. Sales isn't something you try out for a while until something better comes along. Being a student of sales, I take every opportunity to talk to a salesperson when I cross their path.

Years ago, when I was car shopping, the salesperson and I got to talking. I asked how he got into sales. He was almost apologizing for being in sales. He said he was just doing this until something better came along.

At another dealership, looking at another car, I talked to a guy in his early 20s who was making six figures selling cars. He was here to do a job, not waiting for another opportunity to come along.

Success is a mindset! Find it.

Chapter takeaways!

- Sales careers are not built in a day or ruined overnight. They are destroyed because of long-term, consistent activities that fly in the face of logical workflow. Keep this list handy and refer to it regularly to ensure you are not developing any bad habits.
- You're going to hear "No" a lot! Every successful salesperson does. Shrug it off.

- Learn to say "No" yourself. It's one of the key elements of becoming successful.
- Don't half-ass this journey. If you decide on this career, do it like Cortes when he burned his ships (Google it).

Chapter 9

Create Your Own Job

We all think that certain types of people are born to sell. That is simply not true. Selling is as much a science as much as it is an art. It's a completely beatable game when you have a game strategy AND you execute on it.

Jason Stanford
Account Executive Healthcare at Tecsys

William Shakespeare said, "It is not in the stars to hold our destiny but in ourselves." I have often said if I had a time machine, I would go back in time to the late 1500s to early 1600s and throat-punch Shakespeare for talking so weirdly. I went to too many school plays where I didn't know what the hell they were saying...but I digress.

The dude's point is spot on; no one should blame God or some other uncontrollable force for how their life turns out. **You have a certain amount of power to make your life better.** There are ways to work for a better future. While it may be hard and sometimes feel impossible, if you want a perfect job for yourself, why not try to create it?

> **Bill:** What's the craziest thing that's happened in your sales career?
>
> **Jason:** An executive leaving the company one week before the closing on a 15-million-dollar deal that was 1.5 years in the making.

Earlier in the book, I talked about how you can make money from sales without even having a job. That might be too scary. You may like the peace of mind and social aspects that come with working for a company as opposed to working for yourself. Well, there is a way to create your own job that doesn't currently exist with your chosen company!

It's true! I've done it multiple times in my career. You too can go full Build-a-Bear and create the job of your dreams from scratch and then be the one to fill it. Let me tell you how I did it.

Back in the 90s, when I was in the middle of the radio sales portion of my career, I focused on non-traditional revenue. Instead of calling on the typical radio advertisers like car dealers and furniture stores, I sold advertising programs to package good companies and partnered with local outlets like grocery and hardware stores.

The local outlets got free advertising from their suppliers; the suppliers received extra display space and marketing considerations to help them move more product. It was a win-win situation for everyone. Ultimately, I landed in Tulsa to do this work for a radio group and soon added 'recruitment advertising' to the list of programs I developed.

Each commercial started out with a specific message, e.g., "Are you or someone you know a nurse?" Boom, if you were a nurse or knew one, you were going to pay attention to that radio ad!

I loved the direct response aspect of recruitment advertising and the accountability that went with it. Each recruitment commercial had its own phone number to reply to. You knew whether or not the campaign worked simply by seeing if there were any phone calls.

I also created some cool events like drive-thru job fairs where you could drive through a parking lot on the way home to pick up selected job information. Additionally, I introduced virtual job fairs where you could call a number to hear descriptions of open opportunities with both direct companies and staffing firms.

After a while, it dawned on me that I had not met most of my clients in person. Most of the business was done over the phone (the beginning of virtual selling). The company I worked for owned radio stations nationwide, so I proposed we create a 'recruitment advertising division' to create coast-to-coast campaigns.

My current company passed on my proposal, so I contacted a senior VP of Clear Channel Radio—at the time, one of the biggest media companies in the world. I met the VP at a little cafe near his home and proposed a new division that would create a new revenue stream and client base his stations were not currently tapping into. He said yes immediately!

While this 'division' was basically just my starting salary and home office setup, it allowed me to develop campaigns across the country and train other salespeople at sister radio stations on how to go out and get recruitment advertising dollars.

This job didn't exist at Clear Channel. They had no plans at that moment to go after recruitment advertising, but this dope (me), with no college degree and a little chutzpah, had a plan to make them money, and they bought into my idea.

Later on, I partnered with several computing training companies and ran numerous joint recruiting and training events. Two years after I created that job out of thin air, I moved to IT sales because I was hooked on the training industry.

Bill: What's the one piece of advice you would give to someone new to sales?

Jason: Buy Bill's Book ☺. All jokes aside, start with the basic education. If your company doesn't provide sales education, check out Jeffery Gitomer's *Sales Bible*. Buy it. Read it. Practice it.

Go for a walk, leave the headphones at home, and think about what job you would like to have that doesn't currently exist at a company. Then go pitch it.

Chapter takeaways!

- William Shakespeare can be annoying and hard to understand, but sometimes he gets something right.
- If you can't find the perfect sales job to go after, create it yourself.
- Go for a walk. Leave the headphones at home and think about what you really want.

Chapter 10

Final Thoughts

Any change,
even a change for the better
is always accompanied
by drawbacks and discomforts.

Author Arnold Bennett
from the book *The Great Adventure*

So, what have you learned so far? I mean, outside of Bill Becker is kind of a nut job and a grown man who is addicted to Pop-Tarts (frosted brown sugar cinnamon—in case you wanted to thank me for changing your life). Hopefully, you have also learned that sales careers are much different than what you thought before you picked up the book.

Well, I found a new prospect (that's you, in case you were wondering). Throughout the book, I posed questions for you to ask yourself. I used my confidence to persuade you to trust me. Now, I am going for the close! Just like in real life, the close should come naturally. It should be a progression of a chain of events. Finally, you need to ask for the sale. That is what I am going to do. You need to look at a sales career!

Sidebar: Do not make this book a piece of exercise equipment!

You know what I am talking about; you might have a treadmill at home right now that doubles as a place to hang laundry. You had good intentions when you bought the bike or Bowflex, but it just sits in the corner gathering dust. Take action today. Do not let your career gather dust.

If you are tired of constant layoffs or the threat of layoffs, of being ghosted when you apply for a job, or you are currently working but still can't make ends meet after putting in 40+ hours each week, seriously consider switching to a sales career.

The inability to land another job or a better job might reek of failure, but in reality, failure is only giving up. Failure is not considering other options.

As much as I talked about money in this book (because it is important), there are other rewards from a successful sales career. I spent considerable time talking about coworkers and how important they are to your life and career, but it's the same thing with customers. Sure, they represent dollars, but as you build those relationships, some of those customers will become friends. Sometimes those friends like to give you a hard time.

Several years ago, my biggest customers pulled a prank on me. They colluded with my coworkers to make it happen.

It went like this. I was working from home and a coworker called to tell me some cockamamie story about a work package that was delivered to my home by mistake. Said coworker—who shall remain nameless—told me I had to open it while being recorded, just in case something happened to this priceless company package. Yeah, in hindsight that sounds fishy as hell, but at the time, I didn't even second-guess it.

Because I always do what I am told.

I turned on my camera and proceeded to open that damn package. It didn't go well.

Inside the box was this wood crate that was nailed and glued shut like they were protecting the world from Pandora's box and the gates of Hades combined. It was almost impossible to open and took forever! As I grew more and more frustrated, I went full-on Bill Becker mode, getting upset, cussing, and probably throwing a thing or two.

When I finally got it open, I discovered some wonderful gifts from this incredible client. It was a setup! And they had me on video! I apologized profusely for my behavior and choice of language during the next weekly meeting. They just laughed and said that watching me lose my shit was the best part.

Clients become friends. They add richness to your life, sometimes in the form of exasperating pranks.

Job security vs. employment security.

Job security is no longer a reality for most people. Layoffs are in the news every day, and the days of working for a single company and retiring after 40-some years are a relic of the past. Job security relies on a company taking care of you. That your boss likes you. That your company doesn't do something stupid to lose all their customers and go bankrupt.

Employment security is peace of mind. A career in sales will give you employment security. Peace of mind that no matter what happens at your current job, you'll easily find a new one.

It's OK to have doubts when starting a new career, but if you commit and figure shit out along the way…you can build a wonderful career to be proud of! This is a change for you, and as the quote from Arnold Bennett explains, "Not everything will go right and things will feel weird, but the payoff will be worth it."

In the end, selling is like performance art (having conversations). Unlike painting or drawing, or songwriting, this art form can be learned from experience. That experience can begin for you today.

All you have to do is start. I've given you everything you need to know to be able to go get your first sales job. I have shared exactly what I have used in my career. Hopefully, you sat here and thought, "That's it?! I can do that!"

If you are ready to jump in and want additional help, check out my companion course on my website—thejobnobodydreamsof. com. This course offers weekly Q&A sessions with guest lecturers and a virtual mentoring program with me.

Look, starting a new job in an unfamiliar career can be scary and intimidating. Sales is just about having a conversation. You have conversations every day in your life. Now you are just having conversations with prospects and customers.

It's that simple.

Happy selling!

References and Resources

Bennett, A. (1913). *The Great Adventure*. Original Publisher Unknown.

Bernardo, S. (2021, July 20). *2021 Pandemic Grads Are Optimistic About Their Financial Futures Despite Challenging Year*. Business Wire. https://www.businesswire.com/news/home/20210720005232/en/2021-Pandemic-Grads-Are-Optimistic-About-Their-Financial-Futures-Despite-Challenging-Year

Buscemi, S. (1998). *Armageddon* [Film].

Gitomer, J. (1994). *The Sales Bible: The Ultimate Sales Resource*. Buy Wisdom.

Gorman, J. (2018, January 31). *Happiness is Overrated*. Medium. https://medium.com/personal-growth/happiness-is-overrated-3e5fddbf850f

Gretzky, W. *You miss 100% of the shots you don't take*. Source Unknown.

Martin, M. (n.d.). *Silly to be Afraid (Quote)*. Source Unknown.

McNutt III, S. (2022, May 21). *Title Unknown*. Twitter. https://twitter.com/SylvesterMcNutt/status/1505892029955510272?s=20